Editor
Mary S. Jones, M.A.

Editor in Chief
Ina Massler Levin, M.A.

Creative Director
Karen J. Goldfluss, M.S. Ed.

Cover Artist
Barb Lorseyedi

Imaging
Rosa C. See

Publisher

Mary D. Smith, M.S. Ed.

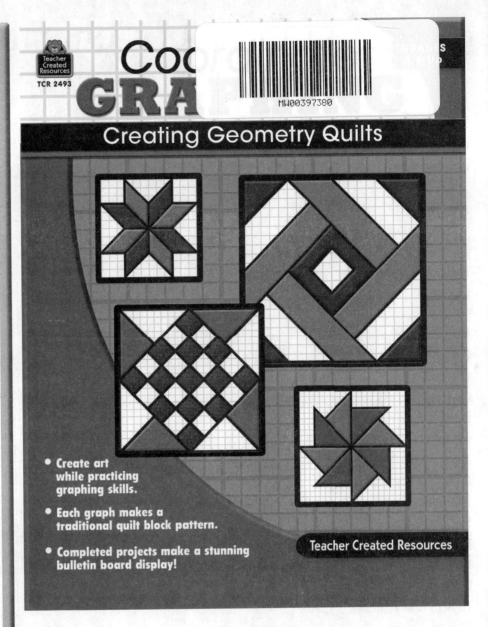

Coordinate GRAPHING

Creating Geometry Quilts

TCR 2493

- Create art while practicing graphing skills.
- Each graph makes a traditional quilt block pattern.
- Completed projects make a stunning bulletin board display!

Teacher Created Resources

Author

Marci Mathers, M.L.I.S.

Teacher Created Resources, Inc.
6421 Industry Way
Westminster, CA 92683
www.teachercreated.com
ISBN: 978-1-4206-2493-9
© 2010 Teacher Created Resources, Inc.
Made in U.S.A.

Teacher Created Resources

Table of Contents

Introduction

How many times have you heard, "When am I ever going to use this in real life?" Probably more times than you care to remember. Are you at a loss for an answer? In reality, math is all around us. It is a part of everyday life, from the intersections (geometry) students cross on the way to school each morning to their shoe sizes (measurement). It can also be part of fun activities, such as the arts and crafts that most students love.

The purpose of *Coordinate Graphing: Creating Geometry Quilts* is to help students create art by using ordered pairs, graph paper, and a straight edge to draw a design. In other words, a math lesson is disguised as an art project. Be sure to have crayons, markers, or colored pencils available.

Finished projects make a stunning bulletin board display that really impresses parents and administrators. Simply cut out the finished designs, staple them to the bulletin board, and "bind" them with 1" or 2" strips of colored construction paper. A word of warning—not all quilt blocks are the same size. If you are planning a bulletin board, try to choose designs with the same dimensions, or cut out all the smaller quilt blocks around the outside edge of the graph paper, leaving a white border.

A Bit About Quilts

Quilts have an interesting history. While many of us consider quilts an art form, they actually started out as a practical way to recycle scrap cloth into a warm blanket. Make an ecology/recycling lesson by assigning your students to think of other scrap materials that might find a useful second life as something else.

Many wonderful websites detail the history of quilts. A few include The Library of Congress http://memory.loc.gov/ammem/qlthtml/qlthome.html and quilt historian Judy Anne Breneman's site http://www.womenfolk.com/historyofquilts/. Challenge your students to find more information on quilts by searching "history of quilts" using an Internet search engine. Have them compare their findings. Is one site better than the other? Why? This is Information Literacy in action!

Some designs are more complicated than others. You can choose to have the entire class work on the same design, or select patterns that best match each student's skill level. Differentiated instruction has never been so user-friendly! Giving each student a different design is also a great technique to prevent copying.

The activities in this book are perfect for a "Fun Friday" project, as a project for half-days or short weeks, or even as a part of your emergency substitute plan kit.

The designs included were sketched from designs posted on Marcia Hohn's quilting website. Some have been slightly modified to work as graphs. Challenge your students to visit Ms. Hohn's website at http://www.quilterscache.com/QuiltBlocksGalore.html to see if they can replicate a design on their own. Have them write the graphing instructions and trade with their classmates.

Teach About Integers

Before having students independently graph points on the coordinate plane, they need a solid knowledge of integers and the number line. Use real-life examples to help your students comprehend negative numbers. For example, you can talk about temperatures as being above zero (positive) or below zero (negative). You can also use the example of money. When you have money, that's a positive amount. When you spend more than what you have and thus owe money, it becomes a negative amount.

Introduction *(cont.)*

Use Correct Terminology

Explain coordinate graphing using the appropriate terms. The *coordinate system* is a method of locating points on a plane in relation to two *perpendicular* number lines. These lines intersect at the *origin* (0,0) and divide the plane into four *quadrants*, or sections. A point is stated as an *ordered pair* (x, y). The first number in the ordered pair tells where to move horizontally along the *x axis*. If it is a positive number, move to the right. If it is a negative number, move to the left.

The second number tells where to move vertically along the *y axis*. If it is positive number, move up the *y* axis. If it is a negative number, move down the *y* axis. Remind students that just as *x* comes before *y* in the alphabet, coordinate points are always listed in *x, y* order. The letter *y* has a tail, which they can associate with the vertical axis.

In Quadrant I, both *x* and *y* have positive values. In Quadrant II, the *x* is negative and the *y* positive. In Quadrant III, both *x* and *y* have negative values, and in Quadrant IV, the *x* is positive while the *y* is negative.

How to Use This Book

To start, make copies of the page you want the students to complete. Then make copies of one of the blank graph paper pages (page 5 or 6) for your students. Graph Paper A shows the positive and negative numerical labels on the *x* and *y* axes up to number 10. Graph Paper B shows the same blank graph, but without any of the numbers showing. All finished quilt blocks will fit inside this large square of graph paper. Some quilt blocks only go up to the number 8 or 9 square.

If possible, make an overhead transparency of the graph paper and display it. Model how to complete one activity, and color in the finished quilt block according to the listed shapes. Be sure to emphasize that students should plot the points in the order given and are not to skip around. Students should use a straight edge to connect the points immediately after plotting each pair of points. Choice of colors has been left to each teacher's discretion. Some suggestions might be to use school colors during Spirit Week, seasonal or holiday colors, or just leave it to each student's imagination and creativity. Have fun and enjoy!

Standards and Benchmarks

The activities in this book meet the following math standards and benchmarks for Level II, which are used with permission from McREL. Copyright 2010 McREL.
Mid–continent Research for Education and Learning, 4601 DTC Boulevard, Suite 500, Denver, CO 80237. Telephone: 303–337–0990. Website: *www.mcrel.org/standards–benchmarks*

Standard 5. Understands and applies basic and advanced properties of the concepts of geometry

1. Knows basic geometric language for describing and naming shapes (e.g., trapezoid, parallelogram, cube, sphere)

Standard 8. Understands and applies basic and advanced properties of functions and algebra

6. Knows basic characteristics and features of the rectangular coordinate system (e.g., the horizontal axis is the X axis and the vertical axis is the Y axis)

Graph Paper A

Name: _____   **Quilt Block Name:** _____

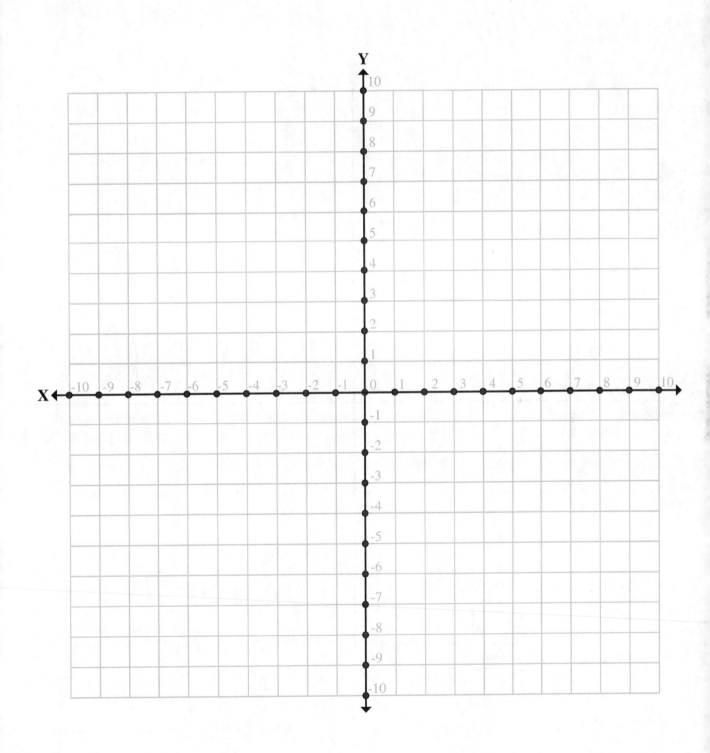

Graph Paper B

Name: _____   **Quilt Block Name:** _____

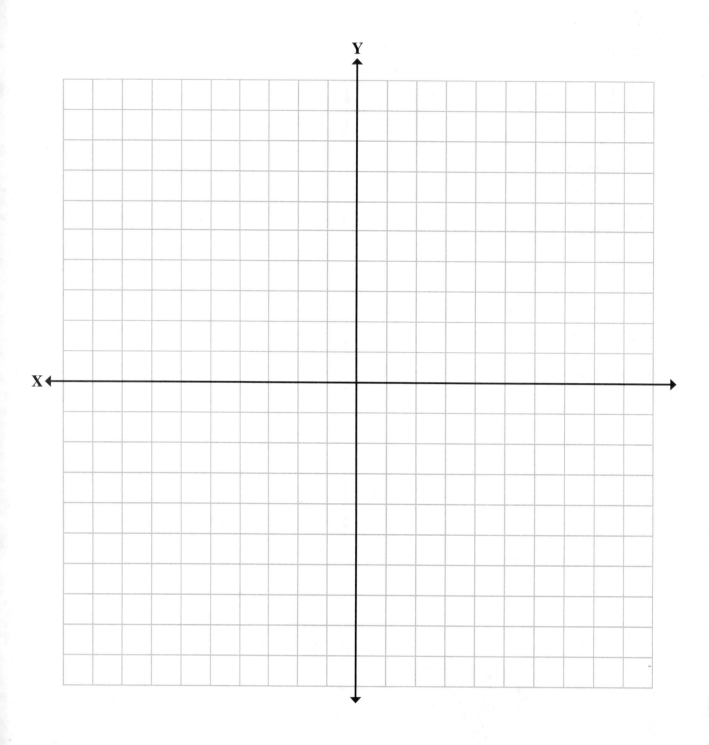

Alaska Homestead

Directions: Find the coordinates indicated below. Work in order, from A to P, connecting each set of points with a straight edge as you go. DO NOT skip around. Use a pencil.

	Connect (X, Y)	To (X, Y)
A	(-10, 10)	(10, 10)
B	(-10, 10)	(-10, -10)
C	(-10, -10)	(10, -10)
D	(10, 10)	(10, -10)
E	(-2, 10)	(-2, -10)
F	(2, 10)	(2, -10)
G	(-10, 2)	(10, 2)
H	(-10, -2)	(10, -2)

	Connect (X, Y)	To (X, Y)
I	(-2, -6)	(2, -6)
J	(-6, 2)	(-6, -2)
K	(-2, 6)	(2, 6)
L	(6, 2)	(6, -2)
M	(-2, 10)	(-10, 2)
N	(-10, -2)	(-2, -10)
O	(2, -10)	(10, -2)
P	(2, 10)	(10, 2)

To see the design, you will need **2 colors**.

Use **color #1** to color the **triangles** with the following coordinates:

1. (-10, 2)   (-2, 2)   (-2, 10)
2. (2, 2)   (2, 10)   (10, 2)
3. (-10, -2)   (-2, -2)   (-2, -10)
4. (2, -2)   (2, -10)   (10, -2)

Use **color #2** to color the **squares** with the following coordinates:

1. (-10, 2)   (-10, -2)   (-6, 2)   (-6, -2)
2. (-2, 2)   (2, 2)   (2, -2)   (-2, -2)
3. (6, 2)   (6, -2)   (10, 2)   (10, -2)
4. (-2, 10)   (-2, 6)   (2, 6)   (2, 10)
5. (-2, -6)   (-2, -10)   (2, -6)   (2, -10)

The finished design is a traditional quilt block called **Alaska Homestead**.

Anvil

Directions: Find the coordinates indicated below. Work in order, from A to N, connecting each set of points with a straight edge as you go. DO NOT skip around. Use a pencil.

	Connect (X, Y)	To (X, Y)
A	(-10, 10)	(10, 10)
B	(-10, 10)	(-10, -10)
C	(-10, -10)	(10, -10)
D	(10, 10)	(10, -10)
E	(-10, 0)	(0, 10)
F	(0, -10)	(10, 0)
G	(0, 5)	(10, 5)
H	(5, 10)	(5, 0)
I	(-5, 0)	(-5, -10)
J	(-10, -5)	(0, -5)
K	(-5, -10)	(0, -5)
L	(-10, -5)	(-5, 0)
M	(0, 5)	(5, 10)
N	(5, 0)	(10, 5)

To see the design, you will need **1 color**.

Color the **squares** with the following coordinates:

1. (-5, 0)   (0, 0)   (0, -5)   (-5, -5)
2. (5, 5)   (5, 0)   (0, 0)   (0, 5)

Color the **triangles** with the following coordinates:

1. (-10, -5)   (-5, -5)   (-5, 0)
2. (-5, -5)   (-5, -10)   (0, -5)
3. (0, 5)   (5, 10)   (5, 5)
4. (5, 0)   (5, 5)   (10, 5)
5. (-10, 0)   (0, 10)   (0, 0)
6. (0, -10)   (10, 0)   (0, 0)

The finished design is a traditional quilt block called **Anvil**.

8

At the Square

Directions: Find the coordinates indicated below. Work in order, from A to X, connecting each set of points with a straight edge as you go. DO NOT skip around. Use a pencil.

	Connect (X, Y)	To (X, Y)
A	(-9, 9)	(-9, -9)
B	(-9, -9)	(9, -9)
C	(9, -9)	(9, 9)
D	(-9, 9)	(9, 9)
E	(-3, 9)	(-3, -9)
F	(3, 9)	(3, -9)
G	(-9, 3)	(9, 3)
H	(-9, -3)	(9, -3)
I	(-9, 9)	(-3, 3)
J	(-9, 3)	(-3, 9)
K	(3, 9)	(9, 3)
L	(3, 3)	(9, 9)

	Connect (X, Y)	To (X, Y)
M	(3, -3)	(9, -9)
N	(3, -9)	(9, -3)
O	(-9, -3)	(-3, -9)
P	(-3, -3)	(-9, -9)
Q	(-3, 7)	(3, 7)
R	(-3, 5)	(3, 5)
S	(7, 3)	(7, -3)
T	(5, 3)	(5, -3)
U	(-3, -5)	(3, -5)
V	(-3, -7)	(3, -7)
W	(-7, 3)	(-7, -3)
X	(-5, 3)	(-5, -3)

To see the design, you will need **1 color**.

Color the **triangles** with the following coordinates:

1. (-9, 9)   (-6, 6)   (-3, 9)
2. (3, 9)   (6, 6)   (9, 9)
3. (-9, 3)   (-6, 6)   (-3, 3)
4. (3, 3)   (6, 6)   (9, 3)
5. (-9, -3)   (-3, -3)   (-6, -6)
6. (3, -3)   (6, -6)   (9, -3)
7. (-9, -9)   (-6, -6)   (-3, -9)
8. (3, -9)   (6, -6)   (9, -9)

Color the **rectangles** with the following coordinates:

1. (-3, 9)   (3, 9)   (3, 7)   (-3, 7)
2. (-3, 5)   (3, 5)   (-3, 3)   (3, 3)
3. (-7, 3)   (-5, 3)   (-5, -3)   (-7, -3)
4. (5, 3)   (7, 3)   (7, -3)   (5, -3)
5. (-3, -3)   (3, -3)   (3, -5)   (-3, -5)
6. (-3, -7)   (3, -7)   (-3, -9)   (3, -9)

The finished design is a traditional quilt block called **At the Square**.

#2493 Coordinate Graphing

Blazing Arrows

Directions: Find the coordinates indicated below. Work in order, from A to R, connecting each set of points with a straight edge as you go. DO NOT skip around. Use a pencil.

	Connect (X, Y)	To (X, Y)
A	(-10, 10)	(10, 10)
B	(-10, 10)	(-10, -10)
C	(-10, -10)	(10, -10)
D	(10, 10)	(10, -10)
E	(-10, 10)	(10, -10)
F	(10, 10)	(-10, -10)
G	(-10, 5)	(10, 5)
H	(-10, -5)	(10, -5)
I	(-5, 10)	(-5, -10)

	Connect (X, Y)	To (X, Y)
J	(5, 10)	(5, -10)
K	(-5, 10)	(0, 5)
L	(5, 10)	(0, 5)
M	(10, 5)	(5, 0)
N	(10, -5)	(5, 0)
O	(5, -10)	(0, -5)
P	(-5, -10)	(0, -5)
Q	(-10, -5)	(-5, 0)
R	(-10, 5)	(-5, 0)

To see the design, you will need **1 color**.

Color the **triangles** with the following coordinates:

1. (-10, 10)   (-5, 10)   (-5, 5)
2. (-5, 10)   (5, 10)   (0, 5)
3. (5, 10)   (10, 10)   (5, 5)
4. (5, 5)   (10, 5)   (5, 0)
5. (5, 0)   (5, -5)   (10, -5)
6. (5, -5)   (5, -10)   (10, -10)
7. (0, -5)   (5, -10)   (-5, -10)
8. (-5, -5)   (-5, -10)   (-10, -10)
9. (-10, -5)   (-5, -5)   (-5, 0)
10. (-10, 5)   (-5, 5)   (-5, 0)
11. (-5, 5)   (0, 0)   (-5, -5)
12. (5, -5)   (0, 0)   (5, 5)

The finished design is a traditional quilt block called **Blazing Arrows**.

Broken Arrows

Directions: Find the coordinates indicated below. Work in order, from A to T, connecting each set of points with a straight edge as you go. DO NOT skip around. Use a pencil.

	Connect (X, Y)	To (X, Y)
A	(-10, 10)	(10, 10)
B	(-10, 10)	(-10, -10)
C	(-10, -10)	(10, -10)
D	(10, 10)	(10, -10)
E	(-2, 10)	(-2, -10)
F	(2, 10)	(2, -10)
G	(-10, 2)	(10, 2)
H	(-10, -2)	(10, -2)
I	(-10, 10)	(-2, 2)
J	(10, 10)	(2, 2)

	Connect (X, Y)	To (X, Y)
K	(10, -10)	(2, -2)
L	(-10, -10)	(-2, -2)
M	(-6, 6)	(-6, -2)
N	(-2, 6)	(6, 6)
O	(6, 2)	(6, -6)
P	(2, -6)	(-6, -6)
Q	(-6, 6)	(-10, 6)
R	(6, 6)	(6, 10)
S	(6, -6)	(10, -6)
T	(-6, -6)	(-6, -10)

To see the design, you will need **1 color**.

Color the **triangles** with the following coordinates:

1. (-10, 10)   (-2, 10)   (-2, 2)
2. (2, 2)   (10, 2)   (10, 10)
3. (2, -2)   (2, -10)   (10, -10)
4. (-10, -2)   (-10, -10)   (-2, -2)

Color the **squares** with the following coordinates:

1. (-2, 6)   (2, 6)   (2, 2)   (-2, 2)
2. (-6, 2)   (-2, 2)   (-2, -2)   (-6, -2)
3. (-2, 2)   (2, 2)   (2, -2)   (-2, -2)
4. (2, 2)   (6, 2)   (6, -2)   (2, -2)
5. (-2, -2)   (2, -2)   (2, -6)   (-2, -6)

The finished design is a traditional quilt block called **Broken Arrows**.

Chevron

Directions: Find the coordinates indicated below. Work in order, from A to V, connecting each set of points with a straight edge as you go. DO NOT skip around. Use a pencil.

	Connect (X, Y)	To (X, Y)
A	(10, 10)	(-10, 10)
B	(-10, 10)	(-10, -10)
C	(-10, -10)	(10, -10)
D	(10, 10)	(10, -10)
E	(-10, 10)	(-5, 5)
F	(-5, 5)	(0, 10)
G	(0, 10)	(5, 5)
H	(5, 5)	(10, 10)
I	(-10, 5)	(-5, 0)
J	(-5, 0)	(0, 5)
K	(0, 5)	(5, 0)

	Connect (X, Y)	To (X, Y)
L	(5, 0)	(10, 5)
M	(-10, 0)	(-5, -5)
N	(-5, -5)	(0, 0)
O	(0, 0)	(5, -5)
P	(5, -5)	(10, 0)
Q	(-10, -5)	(-5,-10)
R	(-5, -10)	(0, -5)
S	(0, -5)	(5, -10)
T	(5, -10)	(10, -5)
U	(-10, 5)	(10, 5)
V	(-10, -5)	(10, -5)

To see the design, you will need **1 color**.

Color the **triangles** with the following coordinates:

1. (-10, 10)   (-10, 5)   (-5, 5)
2. (-10, 5)   (-5, 0)   (0, 5)
3. (-5, 5)   (0, 10)   (5, 5)
4. (5, 5)   (10, 10)   (10, 5)
5. (0, 5)   (5, 0)   (10, 5)
6. (-10, 0)   (-10, -5)   (-5, -5)
7. (-5, -5)   (0, 0)   (5, -5)
8. (5, -5)   (10, 0)   (10, -5)
9. (-10, -5)   (-5, -10)   (0, -5)
10. (0, -5)   (5, -10)   (10, -5)

The finished design is a traditional quilt block called **Chevron**.

Churn Dash

Directions: Find the coordinates indicated below. Work in order, from A to P, connecting each set of points with a straight edge as you go. DO NOT skip around. Use a pencil.

	Connect (X, Y)	To (X, Y)
A	(-10, 10)	(-10, -10)
B	(-10, 10)	(10, 10)
C	(10, 10)	(10, -10)
D	(-10, -10)	(10, -10)
E	(-3, 10)	(-3, -10)
F	(3, 10)	(3, -10)
G	(-10, -3)	(10, -3)
H	(-10, 3)	(10, 3)
I	(-6, 3)	(-6, -3)
J	(6, 3)	(6, -3)
K	(-3, 6)	(3, 6)
L	(-3, -6)	(3, -6)
M	(-10, 3)	(-3, 10)
N	(3, 10)	(10, 3)
O	(3, -10)	(10, -3)
P	(-10, -3)	(-3, -10)

To see the design, you will need **1 color**.

Color the **triangles** with the following coordinates:

1. (3, -10)   (10, -3)   (3, -3)
2. (-10, 3)   (-3, 3)   (-3, 10)
3. (3, 3)   (3, 10)   (10, 3)
4. (-3, -3)   (-3, -10)   (-10, -3)

Color the **rectangles** with the following coordinates:

1. (-6, 3)   (-3, 3)   (-3, -3)   (-6, -3)
2. (-3, 6)   (3, 6)   (3, 3)   (-3, 3)
3. (6, 3)   (6, -3)   (3, -3)   (3, 3)
4. (-3, -3)   (3, -3)   (3, -6)   (-3, -6)

The finished design is a traditional quilt block called **Churn Dash**.

Colonial Pavement

Directions: Find the coordinates indicated below. Work in order, from A to T, connecting each set of points with a straight edge as you go. DO NOT skip around. Use a pencil.

	Connect (X, Y)	To (X, Y)
A	(-8, 8)	(-8, -8)
B	(-8, -8)	(8, -8)
C	(8, -8)	(8, 8)
D	(-8, 8)	(8, 8)
E	(-8, 4)	(-4, 8)
F	(4, 8)	(8, 4)
G	(8, -4)	(4, -8)

	Connect (X, Y)	To (X, Y)
H	(-4, -8)	(-8, -4)
I	(-6, -2)	(0, -8)
J	(-4, 0)	(4, -8)
K	(-2, 0)	(0, -2)
L	(0, 2)	(2, 0)
M	(-4, 8)	(4, 0)
N	(0, 8)	(6, 2)

	Connect (X, Y)	To (X, Y)
O	(-8, 0)	(-2, 6)
P	(-8, -4)	(0, 4)
Q	(-2, 0)	(0, 2)
R	(0, -2)	(2, 0)
S	(0, -4)	(8, 4)
T	(2, -6)	(8, 0)

To see the design, you will need **2 colors**.

Use **color #1** to color the **triangles** with the following coordinates:

1. (-8, 4)   (-8, 8)   (-4, 8)
2. (4, 8)   (8, 8)   (8, 4)
3. (8, -4)   (8, -8)   (4, -8)
4. (-8, -4)   (-8, -8)   (-4, -8)

Use **color #1** to color the **trapezoids** with the following coordinates:

1. (0, 4)   (0, 2)   (-2, 0)   (-4, 0)
2. (-4, 0)   (-2, 0)   (0, -2)   (0, -4)
3. (0, -2)   (0, -4)   (2, 0)   (4, 0)
4. (2, 0)   (4, 0)   (0, 4)   (0, 2)

Use **color #2** to color the **trapezoids** with the following coordinates:

1. (-4, 8)   (0, 8)   (6, 2)   (4, 0)
2. (8, 4)   (8, 0)   (2, -6)   (0, -4)
3. (-4, 0)   (-6, -2)   (0, -8)   (4, -8)
4. (-8, 0)   (-2, 6)   (0, 4)   (-8, -4)

The finished design is a traditional quilt block called **Colonial Pavement**.

Country Checkers

Directions: Find the coordinates indicated below. Work in order, from A to T, connecting each set of points with a straight edge as you go. DO NOT skip around. Use a pencil.

	Connect (X, Y)	To (X, Y)
A	(-10, 10)	(10, 10)
B	(-10, 10)	(-10, -10)
C	(-10, -10)	(10, -10)
D	(10, 10)	(10, -10)
E	(0, 10)	(-10, 0)
F	(-10, 0)	(0, -10)
G	(0, -10)	(10, 0)

	Connect (X, Y)	To (X, Y)
H	(10, 0)	(0, 10)
I	(-5, 5)	(-10, 10)
J	(-5, -5)	(-10, -10)
K	(5, -5)	(10, -10)
L	(5, 5)	(10, 10)
M	(-2, 8)	(8, -2)
N	(-4, 6)	(6, -4)

	Connect (X, Y)	To (X, Y)
O	(-6, 4)	(4, -6)
P	(-8, 2)	(2, -8)
Q	(-8, -2)	(2, 8)
R	(-6, -4)	(4, 6)
S	(-4, -6)	(6, 4)
T	(-2, -8)	(8, 2)

To see the design, you will need **2 colors**.

Use **color #1** to color the **triangles** with the following coordinates:

1. (-10, -10) (-5, -5) (0, -10)
2. (-10, 0) (-10, 10) (-5, 5)
3. (0, 10) (10, 10) (5, 5)
4. (10, 0) (5, -5) (10, -10)

Use **color #2** to color the **rhombuses** with the following coordinates:

1. (0, 10) (2, 8) (-2, 8) (0, 6)
2. (-4, 6) (-2, 4) (-4, 2) (-6, 4)
3. (0, 6) (2, 4) (0, 2) (-2, 4)
4. (2, 4) (4, 6) (6, 4) (4, 2)
5. (-10, 0) (-8, 2) (-6, 0) (-8, -2)
6. (-6, 0) (-4, 2) (-2, 0) (-4, -2)
7. (0, 2) (2, 0) (0, -2) (-2, 0)
8. (2, 0) (4, 2) (6, 0) (4, -2)
9. (6, 0) (8, 2) (10, 0) (8, -2)
10. (-6, -4) (-4, -2) (-2, -4) (-4, -6)
11. (-2, -4) (0, -2) (2, -4) (0, -6)
12. (2, -4) (4, -2) (6, -4) (4, -6)
13. (0, -6) (-2, -8) (0, -10) (2, -8)

The finished design is a traditional quilt block called **Country Checkers.**

Crazy Anne

Directions: Find the coordinates indicated below. Work in order, from A to X, connecting each set of points with a straight edge as you go. DO NOT skip around. Use a pencil.

	Connect (X, Y)	To (X, Y)
A	(-10, 10)	(10, 10)
B	(-10, -10)	(10, -10)
C	(-10, 10)	(-10, -10)
D	(10, -10)	(10, 10)
E	(-10, 6)	(-6, 6)
F	(-6, 6)	(-6, 10)
G	(6, 6)	(10, 6)
H	(6, 6)	(6, 10)

	Connect (X, Y)	To (X, Y)
I	(6, -10)	(6, -6)
J	(6, -6)	(10, -6)
K	(-6, -10)	(-6, -6)
L	(-6, -6)	(-10, -6)
M	(-10, 2)	(10, 2)
N	(-10, -2)	(10, -2)
O	(-2, 10)	(-2, -10)
P	(2, 10)	(2, -10)

	Connect (X, Y)	To (X, Y)
Q	(-10, 2)	(-2, 10)
R	(-2, 2)	(2, 10)
S	(10, 2)	(2, 10)
T	(10, -2)	(2, 2)
U	(10, -2)	(2, -10)
V	(-2, -10)	(2, -2)
W	(-2, -10)	(-10, -2)
X	(-10, 2)	(-2, -2)

To see the design, you will need **3 colors**.

Use **color #1** to color the **squares** with the following coordinates:

1. (2, 2)   (2, -2)   (-2, -2)   (-2, 2)
2. (-10, 10)   (-6, 10)   (-6, 6)   (-10, 6)
3. (-10, -6)   (-6, -6)   (-10, -10)   (-6, -10)
4. (6, 6)   (6, 10)   (10, 6)   (10, 10)
5. (6, -6)   (10, -6)   (6, -10)   (10, -10)

Use **color #2** to color the **triangles** with the following coordinates:

1. (-10, -2)   (-2, -2)   (-2, -10)
2. (2, -2)   (2, -10)   (10, -2)
3. (2, 10)   (2, 2)   (10, 2)
4. (-10, 2)   (-2, 2)   (-2, 10)

Use **color #3** to color the **triangles** with the following coordinates:

1. (2, 10)   (-2, 2)   (2, 2)
2. (2, 2)   (2, -2)   (10, -2)
3. (-2, -2)   (2, -2)   (-2, -10)
4. (-10, 2)   (-2, 2)   (-2, -2)

The finished design is a traditional quilt block called **Crazy Anne.**

Crossed Roads

Directions: Find the coordinates indicated below. Work in order, from A to BB, connecting each set of points with a straight edge as you go. DO NOT skip around. Use a pencil.

	Connect (X, Y)	To (X, Y)		Connect (X, Y)	To (X, Y)		Connect (X, Y)	To (X, Y)
A	(-10, 10)	(10, 10)	**K**	(-10, -4)	(10, -4)	**T**	(10, 0)	(6, -4)
B	(-10, 10)	(-10, -10)	**L**	(-10, -6)	(10, -6)	**U**	(4, -6)	(0, -10)
C	(-10, -10)	(10, -10)	**M**	(-4, 0)	(0, 4)	**V**	(0, -10)	(-4, -6)
D	(10, 10)	(10, -10)	**N**	(0, 4)	(4, 0)	**W**	(-10, 0)	(-6, -4)
E	(-6, 10)	(-6, -10)	**O**	(4, 0)	(0, -4)	**X**	(-6, 4)	(-10, 0)
F	(-4, 10)	(-4, -10)	**P**	(0, -4)	(-4, 0)	**Y**	(-10, 6)	(-6, 10)
G	(4, 10)	(4, -10)	**Q**	(-4, 6)	(0, 10)	**Z**	(6, 10)	(10, 6)
H	(6, 10)	(6, -10)	**R**	(0, 10)	(4, 6)	**AA**	(10, -6)	(6, -10)
I	(-10, 6)	(10, 6)	**S**	(6, 4)	(10, 0)	**BB**	(-10, -6)	(-6, -10)
J	(-10, 4)	(10, 4)						

To see the design, you will need **3 colors**.

Use **color #1** to color the **rhombus** with the following coordinates:

1. (-4, 0)   (0, 4)   (4, 0)   (0, -4)

Use **color #1** to color the **triangles** with the following coordinates:

1. (-10, 6)   (-10, 10)   (-6, 10)
2. (6, 10)   (10, 10)   (10, 6)
3. (10, -6)   (10, -10)   (6, -10)
4. (-10, -10)   (-6, -10)   (-10, -6)

Use **color #2** to color the **triangles** with the following coordinates:

1. (0, 10)   (4, 6)   (-4, 6)   5. (-4, 0)   (-4, 4)   (0, 4)
2. (6, 4)   (10, 0)   (6, -4)   6. (0, 4)   (4, 4)   (4, 0)
3. (4, -6)   (0, -10)   (-4, -6)   7. (4, 0)   (4, -4)   (0, -4)
4. (-10, 0)   (-6, -4)   (-6, 4)   8. (-4, 0)   (-4, -4)   (0, -4)

Use **color #3** to color the **rectangles** with the following coordinates:

1. (-6, 10)   (-4, 10)   (-4, -10)   (-6, -10)
2. (4, 10)   (6, 10)   (6, -10)   (4, -10)
3. (-10, 6)   (10, 6)   (10, 4)   (-10, 4)
4. (-10, -4)   (10, -4)   (10, -6)   (-10, -6)

The finished design is a traditional quilt block called **Crossed Roads**.

Double Quartet

Directions: Find the coordinates indicated below. Work in order, from A to N, connecting each set of points with a straight edge as you go. DO NOT skip around. Use a pencil.

	Connect (X, Y)	To (X, Y)
A	(-8, 8)	(-8, -8)
B	(-8, -8)	(8, -8)
C	(8, -8)	(8, 8)
D	(-8, 8)	(8, 8)
E	(-4, 8)	(-4, -8)
F	(4, 8)	(4, -8)
G	(-8, 4)	(8, 4)

	Connect (X, Y)	To (X, Y)
H	(-8, -4)	(8, -4)
I	(-4, 4)	(4, -4)
J	(4, 4)	(-4, -4)
K	(-4, 4)	(0, 8)
L	(4, 4)	(8, 0)
M	(4, -4)	(0, -8)
N	(-8, 0)	(-4, -4)

To see the design you will need **2 colors**.

Use **color #1** to color the **triangles** with the following coordinates:

1. (-4, 4)   (0, 8)   (0, 4)
2. (-4, 0)   (-4, 4)   (0, 0)
3. (0, 0)   (0, 4)   (4, 4)
4. (4, 0)   (4, 4)   (8, 0)
5. (-8, 0)   (-4, -4)   (-4, 0)
6. (0, 0)   (0, -4)   (-4, -4)
7. (0, 0)   (4, 0)   (4, -4)
8. (0, -4)   (4, -4)   (0, -8)

Use **color #2** to color the **squares** with the following coordinates:

1. (-8, 4)   (-8, 8)   (-4, 8)   (-4, 4)
2. (4, 8)   (8, 8)   (8, 4)   (4, 4)
3. (-8, -4)   (-8, -8)   (-4, -8)   (-4, -4)
4. (4, -4)   (8, -4)   (8, -8)   (4, -8)

The finished design is a traditional quilt block called **Double Quartet**.

Dove in a Window

Directions: Find the coordinates indicated below. Work in order, from A to FF, connecting each set of points with a straight edge as you go. DO NOT skip around. Use a pencil.

	Connect (X, Y)	To (X, Y)
A	(-10, 10)	(10, 10)
B	(-10, 10)	(-10, -10)
C	(-10, -10)	(10, -10)
D	(10, 10)	(10, -10)
E	(-10, 1)	(10, 1)
F	(-10, -1)	(10, -1)
G	(-1, 10)	(-1, -10)
H	(1, 10)	(1, -10)
I	(-10, 1)	(-1, 10)
J	(1, 10)	(10, 1)
K	(10, -1)	(1, -10)

	Connect (X, Y)	To (X, Y)
L	(-1, -10)	(-10, -1)
M	(-7, 10)	(-7, 4)
N	(-10, 7)	(-4, 7)
O	(-10, 4)	(-4, 10)
P	(-4, 10)	(-4, 7)
Q	(-10, 4)	(-7, 4)
R	(7, 10)	(7, 4)
S	(4, 7)	(10, 7)
T	(4, 10)	(10, 4)
U	(4, 7)	(4, 10)
V	(7, 4)	(10, 4)

	Connect (X, Y)	To (X, Y)
W	(7, -4)	(7, -10)
X	(4, -7)	(10, -7)
Y	(4, -10)	(10, -4)
Z	(4, -7)	(4, -10)
AA	(7, -4)	(10, -4)
BB	(-7, -4)	(-7, -10)
CC	(-10, -7)	(-4, -7)
DD	(-10, -4)	(-4, -10)
EE	(-4, -7)	(-4, -10)
FF	(-10, -4)	(-7, -4)

To see the design, you will need **3 colors**.

Use **color #1** to color the **square** with the following coordinates:

1. (-1, 1)   (1, 1)   (1, -1)   (-1, -1)

Use **color #2** to color the **rectangles** with the following coordinates:

1. (-1, 10)   (1, 10)   (1, 1)   (-1, 1)   3. (-10, 1)   (-1, 1)   (-1, -1)   (-10, -1)
2. (-1, -1)   (1, -1)   (1, -10) (-1, -10)   4. (1, 1)   (10, 1)   (10, -1)   (1, -1)

Use **color #3** to color the **squares** with the following coordinates:

1. (-10, 10) (-7, 10) (-7, 7)   (-10, 7)   3. (7, -7)   (10, -7)   (10, -10) (7, -10)
2. (7, 10)   (10, 10) (10, 7)   (7, 7)   4. (-10, -10) (-10, -7) (-7, -7)   (-7, -10)

Use **color #3** to color the **triangles** with the following coordinates:

1. (-10, 4)   (-7, 4)   (-7, 7)   7. (-10, -4) (-7, -4)   (-7, -7)
2. (-7, 7)   (-4, 7)   (-4, 10)   8. (-7, -7)   (-4, -7)   (-4, -10)
3. (4, 10)   (4, 7)   (7, 7)   9. (-10, 1)   (-1, 1)   (-1, 10)
4. (7, 7)   (7, 4)   (10, 4)   10. (1, 10)   (1, 1)   (10, 1)
5. (7, -4)   (7, -7)   (10, -4)   11. (1, -1)   (1, -10)   (10, -1)
6. (4, -7)   (4, -10) (7, -7)   12. (-10, -1) (-1, -1)   (-1, -10)

The finished design is a traditional quilt block called **Dove in a Window**.

Dutch Nine Patch

Directions: Find the coordinates indicated below. Work in order, from A to L, connecting each set of points with a straight edge as you go. DO NOT skip around. Use a pencil.

	Connect (X, Y)	To (X, Y)
A	(-9, 9)	(-9, -9)
B	(-9, -9)	(9, -9)
C	(9, -9)	(9, 9)
D	(-9, 9)	(9, 9)
E	(-3, 9)	(-3, -9)
F	(3, 9)	(3, -9)
G	(-9, 3)	(9, 3)
H	(-9, -3)	(9, -3)
I	(-1, 3)	(-1, -3)
J	(1, 3)	(1, -3)
K	(-3, 1)	(3, 1)
L	(-3, -1)	(3, -1)

To see the design, you will need **1 color**.

Color the **squares** with the following coordinates:

1. (-3, 3)   (-1, 3)   (-1, 1)   (-3, 1)
2. (1, 3)   (3, 3)   (3, 1)   (1, 1)
3. (-1, 1)   (1, 1)   (1, -1)   (-1, -1)
4. (-3, -1)   (-3, -3)   (-1, -3)   (-1, -1)
5. (1, -1)   (3, -1)   (3, -3)   (1, -3)
6. (-9, 9)   (-3, 9)   (-3, 3)   (-9, 3)
7. (3, 9)   (9, 9)   (3, 3)   (9, 3)
8. (3, -3)   (9, -3)   (9, -9)   (3, -9)
9. (-9, -3)   (-3, -3)   (-3, -9)   (-9, -9)

The finished design is a traditional quilt block called **Dutch Nine Patch**.

Dutchman's Puzzle

Directions: Find the coordinates indicated below. Work in order, from A to V, connecting each set of points with a straight edge as you go. DO NOT skip around. Use a pencil.

	Connect (X, Y)	To (X, Y)
A	(-10, 10)	(10, 10)
B	(-10, -10)	(10, -10)
C	(-10, 10)	(-10, -10)
D	(10, 10)	(10, -10)
E	(-5, 5)	(5, -5)
F	(-5, -5)	(5, 5)
G	(-10, 0)	(-5, 5)
H	(-10, 5)	(0, 5)
I	(-10, 5)	(-5, 10)
J	(-5, 10)	(0, 5)
K	(5, 5)	(0, 10)

	Connect (X, Y)	To (X, Y)
L	(5, 0)	(5, 10)
M	(5, 10)	(10, 5)
N	(5, 0)	(10, 5)
O	(5, -5)	(10, 0)
P	(0, -5)	(10, -5)
Q	(0, -5)	(5, -10)
R	(5, -10)	(10, -5)
S	(-10, -5)	(-5, 0)
T	(-10, -5)	(-5, -10)
U	(-5, -5)	(0, -10)
V	(-5, 0)	(-5, -10)

To see the design, you will need **1 color**.

Color the **triangles** with the following coordinates:

1. (-5, 10)   (0, 5)   (-10, 5)
2. (0, 0)   (-5, 5)   (-10, 0)
3. (5, 0)   (5, 10)   (10, 5)
4. (0, 0)   (0, 10)   (5, 5)
5. (-5, 0)   (-5, -10) (-10, -5)
6. (0, 0)   (-5, -5)   (0, -10)
7. (0, 0)   (10, 0)   (5, -5)
8. (0, -5)   (10, -5)   (5, -10)

The finished design is a traditional quilt block called **Dutchman's Puzzle**.

Fool's Square

Directions: Find the coordinates indicated below. Work in order, from A to X, connecting each set of points with a straight edge as you go. DO NOT skip around. Use a pencil.

	Connect (X, Y)	To (X, Y)
A	(-10, 10)	(10, 10)
B	(-10, 10)	(-10, -10)
C	(-10, -10)	(10, -10)
D	(10, 10)	(10, -10)
E	(-6, 10)	(-6, -10)
F	(-2, 10)	(-2, -10)
G	(2, 10)	(2, -10)
H	(6, 10)	(6, -10)

	Connect (X, Y)	To (X, Y)
I	(-10, 6)	(10, 6)
J	(-10, 2)	(10, 2)
K	(-10, -2)	(10, -2)
L	(-10, -6)	(10, -6)
M	(-2, 6)	(-6, 10)
N	(-6, 2)	(-10, 6)
O	(-10, 6)	(-6, 10)
P	(-6, -2)	(-10, -6)

	Connect (X, Y)	To (X, Y)
Q	(-10, -6)	(-6, -10)
R	(-6, -10)	(-2, -6)
S	(2, -6)	(6, -10)
T	(6, -2)	(10, -6)
U	(6, -10)	(10, -6)
V	(2, 6)	(6, 10)
W	(6, 2)	(10, 6)
X	(6, 10)	(10, 6)

To see the design, you will need **1 color**.

Color the **triangles** with the following coordinates:

1. (-2, 6)   (-6, 10)   (-6, 6)
2. (-6, 2)   (-10, 6)   (-6, 6)
3. (6, 2)   (6, 6)   (10, 6)
4. (2, 6)   (6, 10)   (6, 6)
5. (6, -2)   (6, -6)   (10, -6)
6. (2, -6)   (6, -6)   (6, -10)
7. (-2, -6)   (-6, -10)   (-6, -6)
8. (-6, -2)   (-6, -6)   (-10, -6)
9. (-10, 6)   (-10, 10)   (-6, 10)
10. (6, 10)   (10, 10)   (10, 6)
11. (6, -10)   (10, -6)   (10, -10)
12. (-6, -10)   (-10, -10)   (-10, -6)

Color the **squares** with the following coordinates:

1. (-6, 2)   (-2, 2)   (-2, -2)   (-6, -2)
2. (2, 2)   (6, 2)   (6, -2)   (2, -2)
3. (-2, 6)   (2, 6)   (2, 2)   (-2, 2)
4. (-2, -6)   (2, -6)   (2, -2)   (-2, -2)

The finished design is a traditional quilt block called **Fool's Square**.

Four Goblets

Directions: Find the coordinates indicated below. Work in order, from A to JJ, connecting each set of points with a straight edge as you go. DO NOT skip around. Use a pencil.

	Connect (X, Y)	To (X, Y)
A	(-9, 9)	(-9, -9)
B	(-9, -9)	(9, -9)
C	(9, -9)	(9, 9)
D	(-9, 9)	(9, 9)
E	(-3, 9)	(-3, -9)
F	(3, 9)	(3, -9)
G	(-9, 3)	(9, 3)
H	(-9, -3)	(9, -3)
I	(0, 3)	(3, 0)
J	(3, 0)	(0, -3)
K	(0, -3)	(-3, 0)
L	(-3, 0)	(0, 3)

	Connect (X, Y)	To (X, Y)
M	(-6, 9)	(-3, 6)
N	(-3, 6)	(-6, 3)
O	(-6, 3)	(-9, 6)
P	(-9, 6)	(-6, 9)
Q	(3, 6)	(6, 9)
R	(6, 9)	(9, 6)
S	(9, 6)	(6, 3)
T	(6, 3)	(3, 6)
U	(-6, -3)	(-3, -6)
V	(-3, -6)	(-6, -9)
W	(-6, -9)	(-9, -6)
X	(-9, -6)	(-6, -3)

	Connect (X, Y)	To (X, Y)
Y	(6, -3)	(9, -6)
Z	(9, -6)	(6, -9)
AA	(6, -9)	(3, -6)
BB	(3, -6)	(6, -3)
CC	(-4, 3)	(-3, 2)
DD	(-3, 4)	(-2, 3)
EE	(2, 3)	(3, 4)
FF	(3, 2)	(4, 3)
GG	(-3, -2)	(-4, -3)
HH	(-2, -3)	(-3, -4)
II	(2, -3)	(3, -4)
JJ	(3, -2)	(4, -3)

To see the design, you will need **1 color**.

Color the **triangles** with the following coordinates:

1. (-9, 6) (-9, 9) (-6, 9)
2. (-6, 9) (-3, 9) (-3, 6)
3. (-9, 6) (-9, 3) (-6, 3)
4. (3, 6) (3, 9) (6, 9)
5. (6, 9) (9, 9) (9, 6)
6. (6, 3) (9, 3) (9, 6)
7. (-9, -3) (-6, -3) (-9, -6)
8. (-9, -6) (-9, -9) (-6, -9)
9. (-6, -9) (-3, -9) (-3, -6)
10. (3, -6) (3, -9) (6, -9)
11. (6, -9) (9, -9) (9, -6)
12. (6, -3) (9, -3) (9, -6)

Color the **polygons** with the following coordinates:

1. (-3, 9) (-3, 4) (-2, 3) (2, 3) (3, 4) (3, 9)
2. (-9, 3) (-4, 3) (-3, 2) (-3, -2) (-4, -3) (-9, -3)
3. (3, 2) (4, 3) (9, 3) (9, -3) (4, -3) (3, -2)
4. (-3, -4) (-2, -3) (2, -3) (3, -4) (3, -9) (-3, -9)

Color the **rhombus** with the following coordinates:

1. (0, 3) (3, 0) (0, -3) (-3, 0)

The finished design is a traditional quilt block called **Four Goblets**.

Framed Four Patch

Directions: Find the coordinates indicated below. Work in order, from A to H, connecting each set of points with a straight edge as you go. DO NOT skip around. Use a pencil.

	Connect (X, Y)	To (X, Y)
A	(-8, -8)	(-8, 8)
B	(-8, 8)	(8, 8)
C	(8, 8)	(8, -8)
D	(8, -8)	(-8, -8)
E	(-4, 8)	(-4, -8)
F	(4, 8)	(4, -8)
G	(-4, 4)	(4, 4)
H	(-4, -4)	(4, -4)

To see the design, you will need **3 colors**.

Use **color #1** to color the **squares** with the following coordinates:

1. (-4, 0)   (0, 0)   (0, -4)   (-4, -4)
2. (0, 0)   (0, 4)   (4, 4)   (4, 0)

Use **color #2** to color the **squares** with the following coordinates:

1. (-4, 0)   (-4, 4)   (0, 4)   (0, 0)
2. (0, 0)   (4, 0)   (4, -4)   (0, -4)

Use **color #3** to color the **rectangles** with the following coordinates:

1. (-8, -8)   (-8, 8)   (-4, 8)   (-4, -8)
2. (-4, 4)   (-4, 8)   (4, 8)   (4, 4)
3. (4, 8)   (8, 8)   (8, -8)   (4, -8)
4. (-4, -8)   (-4, -4)   (4, -4)   (4, -8)

The finished design is a traditional quilt block called **Framed Four Patch**.

Fruit Basket

Directions: Find the coordinates indicated below. Work in order, from A to U, connecting each set of points with a straight edge as you go. DO NOT skip around. Use a pencil.

	Connect (X, Y)	To (X, Y)
A	(-10, 10)	(-10, -10)
B	(-10, -10)	(10, -10)
C	(10, -10)	(10, 10)
D	(-10, 10)	(10, 10)
E	(-10, -6)	(2, -6)
F	(-6, -2)	(10, -2)
G	(-10, 2)	(10, 2)

	Connect (X, Y)	To (X, Y)
H	(-10, 6)	(10, 6)
I	(-6, 10)	(-6, -6)
J	(-2, -6)	(-2, 10)
K	(2, -10)	(2, 6)
L	(6, -2)	(6, 10)
M	(2, -10)	(10, -2)
N	(-2, -6)	(6, 2)

	Connect (X, Y)	To (X, Y)
O	(-6, -6)	(6, 6)
P	(-10, -6)	(6, 10)
Q	(-6, 2)	(-2, 6)
R	(-10, 6)	(-6, 2)
S	(-6, 10)	(-2, 6)
T	(-10, 2)	(-6, -2)
U	(-2, 10)	(2, 6)

To see the design, you will need **2 colors**.

Use **color #1** (*Hint:* use the color of a fruit) to color the **triangles** with the following coordinates:

1. (-10, 6)   (-6, 6)   (-6, 2)
2. (-6, 6)   (-6, 10)   (-2, 6)
3. (-2, 10)   (2, 6)   (-2, 6)
4. (-2, 6)   (-6, 2)   (-2, -2)
5. (-6, 2)   (-10, 2)   (-6, -2)

Use **color #2** (*Hint:* use the color of a basket) to color the **triangles** with the following coordinates:

1. (2, -10)   (10, -2)   (2, -2)
2. (-2, -6)   (2, -6)   (2, -2)
3. (2, -2)   (6, -2)   (6, 2)
4. (-6, -6)   (-2, -6)   (-2, -2)
5. (2, 2)   (6, 2)   (6, 6)
6. (-10, -6)   (-6, -6)   (-6, -2)
7. (-6, -2)   (-2, 2)   (-2, -2)
8. (-2, 2)   (2, 6)   (2, 2)
9. (2, 6)   (6, 6)   (6, 10)
10. (-2, -2)   (2, -2)   (2, 2)

The finished design is a traditional quilt block called **Fruit Basket**.

Grandmother's Puzzle

Directions: Find the coordinates indicated below. Work in order, from A to T, connecting each set of points with a straight edge as you go. DO NOT skip around. Use a pencil.

	Connect (X, Y)	To (X, Y)
A	(-10, -10)	(-10, 10)
B	(-10, 10)	(10, 10)
C	(10, 10)	(10, -10)
D	(10, -10)	(-10, -10)
E	(-6, 10)	(-6, -2)
F	(-6, -6)	(-6, -10)
G	(-2, 2)	(-2, -10)
H	(2, 10)	(2, -2)
I	(6, 10)	(6, 6)
J	(6, 2)	(6, -10)

	Connect (X, Y)	To (X, Y)
K	(-10, 6)	(2, 6)
L	(6, 6)	(10, 6)
M	(-2, 2)	(10, 2)
N	(-10, -2)	(2, -2)
O	(-10, -6)	(-6, -6)
P	(-2, -6)	(10, -6)
Q	(-10, -2)	(-2, -10)
R	(-6, -2)	(2, 6)
S	(2, 10)	(10, 2)
T	(-2, -6)	(6, 2)

To see the design, you will need **2 colors**.

Use **color #1** to color the **squares** with the following coordinates:

1. (-10, 6)   (-10, 10)   (-6, 10)   (-6, 6)
2. (6, 6)   (6, 10)   (10, 10)   (10, 6)
3. (-2, 2)   (2, 2)   (2, -2)   (-2, -2)
4. (-10, -6)   (-6, -6)   (-6, -10)   (-10, -10)
5. (6, -6)   (10, -6)   (10, -10)   (6, -10)

Use **color #2** to color the **triangles** with the following coordinates:

1. (-6, 6)   (-6, -2)   (2, 6)
2. (2, 10)   (10, 2)   (2, 2)
3. (-10, -2)   (-2, -2)   (-2, -10)
4. (-2, -6)   (6, -6)   (6, 2)

The finished design is a traditional quilt block called **Grandmother's Puzzle**.

Hearth and Home

Directions: Find the coordinates indicated below. Work in order, from A to V, connecting each set of points with a straight edge as you go. DO NOT skip around. Use a pencil.

	Connect (X, Y)	To (X, Y)
A	(-10, 10)	(10, 10)
B	(-10, 10)	(-10, -10)
C	(-10, -10)	(10, -10)
D	(10, 10)	(10, -10)
E	(-6, 10)	(-6, -10)
F	(-2, 10)	(-2, -10)
G	(2, 10)	(2, -10)
H	(6, 10)	(6, -10)

	Connect (X, Y)	To (X, Y)
I	(-10, 6)	(10, 6)
J	(-10, 2)	(-2, 2)
K	(2, 2)	(10, 2)
L	(-10, -2)	(-2, -2)
M	(2, -2)	(10, -2)
N	(-10, -6)	(10, -6)
O	(-10, 6)	(-6, 2)

	Connect (X, Y)	To (X, Y)
P	(-6, 10)	(-2, 6)
Q	(2, 6)	(6, 10)
R	(6, 2)	(10, 6)
S	(6, -2)	(10, -6)
T	(2, -6)	(6, -10)
U	(-6, -10)	(-2, -6)
V	(-10, -6)	(-6, -2)

To see the design, you will need **1 color**.

Color the **triangles** with the following coordinates:

1. (-6, 6)   (-6, 10)   (-2, 6)
2. (2, 6)   (6, 10)   (6, 6)
3. (-10, 6)   (-6, 6)   (-6, 2)
4. (6, 6)   (10, 6)   (6, 2)
5. (-10, -6)   (-6, -2)   (-6, -6)
6. (6, -2)   (6, -6)   (10, -6)
7. (-6, -6)   (-2, -6)   (-6, -10)
8. (2, -6)   (6, -6)   (6, -10)

Color the **squares** with the following coordinates:

1. (-2, 10)   (2, 10)   (2, 6)   (-2, 6)
2. (-6, 6)   (-2, 6)   (-2, 2)   (-6, 2)
3. (2, 6)   (6, 6)   (6, 2)   (2, 2)
4. (-10, 2)   (-6, 2)   (-6, -2)   (-10, -2)
5. (6, 2)   (10, 2)   (10, -2)   (6, -2)
6. (-6, -2)   (-2, -2)   (-2, -6)   (-6, -6)
7. (2, -2)   (6, -2)   (6, -6)   (2, -6)
8. (-2, -6)   (2, -6)   (2, -10)   (-2, -10)

The finished design is a traditional quilt block called **Hearth and Home**.

Hill and Valley

Directions: Find the coordinates indicated below. Work in order, from A to R, connecting each set of points with a straight edge as you go. DO NOT skip around. Use a pencil.

	Connect (X, Y)	To (X, Y)
A	(-10, 10)	(10, 10)
B	(-10, 10)	(-10, -10)
C	(-10, -10)	(10, -10)
D	(10, -10)	(10, 10)
E	(-10, 0)	(0, 10)
F	(0, 10)	(10, 0)
G	(-10, -10)	(0, 0)
H	(0, 0)	(10, -10)
I	(-4, 0)	(-4, 6)
J	(4, 0)	(4, 6)
K	(-4, 6)	(4, 0)
L	(-4, -4)	(4, -4)
M	(-4, -4)	(-4, -10)
N	(-4, -10)	(4, -4)
O	(-4, 0)	(4, 6)
P	(-4, 6)	(4, 6)
Q	(-4, -4)	(4, -10)
R	(4, -4)	(4, -10)

To see the design, you will need **1 color**.

Color the **triangles** with the following coordinates:

1. (-10, 0)   (-4, 6)   (-4, 0)
2. (-4, 0)   (4, 0)   (0, 3)
3. (-4, 6)   (4, 6)   (0, 3)
4. (-4, 6)   (0, 10)   (4, 6)
5. (4, 0)   (4, 6)   (10, 0)
6. (0, 0)   (-4, -4)   (4, -4)
7. (-4, -10)   (4, -10)   (0, -7)
8. (0, -7)   (4, -4)   (-4, -4)
9. (-10, -10)   (-4, -10)   (-4, -4)
10. (4, -4)   (4, -10)   (10, -10)

The finished design is a traditional quilt block called **Hill and Valley**.

Interlocked Squares

Directions: Find the coordinates indicated below. Work in order, from A to L, connecting each set of points with a straight edge as you go. DO NOT skip around. Use a pencil.

	Connect (X, Y)	To (X, Y)
A	(-9, 9)	(-9, -9)
B	(-9, -9)	(9, -9)
C	(9, -9)	(9, 9)
D	(-9, 9)	(9, 9)
E	(-3, 3)	(9, 3)
F	(3, 3)	(3, -9)
G	(3, -3)	(-9, -3)
H	(-3, -3)	(-3, 9)
I	(6, 0)	(6, -9)
J	(0, -6)	(-9, -6)
K	(-6, 0)	(-6, 9)
L	(0, 6)	(9, 6)

To see the design, you will need **2 colors**.

Use **color #1** to color the **square** with the following coordinates:

1. (-3, 3)   (-3, -3)   (3, 3)   (3, -3)

Use **color #1** to color the **rectangles** with the following coordinates:

1. (-9, 9)   (-6, 9)   (-6, 0)   (-9, 0)
2. (0, 9)   (0, 6)   (9, 9)   (9, 6)
3. (6, 0)   (9, 0)   (9, -9)   (6, -9)
4. (-9, -9)   (-9, -6)   (0, -6)   (0, -9)

Use **color #2** to color the **rectangles** with the following coordinates:

1. (-6, 9)   (-3, 9)   (-3, 0)   (-6, 0)
2. (0, 6)   (9, 6)   (9, 3)   (0, 3)
3. (3, 0)   (6, 0)   (6, -9)   (3, -9)
4. (-9, -3)   (-9, -6)   (0, -3)   (0, -6)

The finished design is a traditional quilt block called **Interlocked Squares**.

Memory

Directions: Find the coordinates indicated below. Work in order, from A to BB, connecting each set of points with a straight edge as you go. DO NOT skip around. Use a pencil.

	Connect (X, Y)	To (X, Y)
A	(-9, 9)	(-9, -9)
B	(-9, -9)	(9, -9)
C	(9, -9)	(9, 9)
D	(-9, 9)	(9, 9)
E	(-6, -9)	(-6, 9)
F	(-3, -9)	(-3, 9)
G	(3, -9)	(3, 9)
H	(6, -9)	(6, 9)
I	(-9, 6)	(9, 6)
J	(-9, 3)	(9, 3)

	Connect (X, Y)	To (X, Y)
K	(-9, -3)	(9, -3)
L	(-9, -6)	(9, -6)
M	(-9, 3)	(-6, 0)
N	(-6, 0)	(-9, -3)
O	(-9, -6)	(-3, 0)
P	(-9, 6)	(-3, 0)
Q	(-3, 9)	(0, 6)
R	(3, 9)	(0, 6)
S	(-6, 9)	(0, 3)

	Connect (X, Y)	To (X, Y)
T	(6, 9)	(0, 3)
U	(9, 3)	(6, 0)
V	(9, -3)	(6, 0)
W	(9, 6)	(3, 0)
X	(9, -6)	(3, 0)
Y	(6, -9)	(0, -3)
Z	(-6, -9)	(0, -3)
AA	(-3, -9)	(0, -6)
BB	(3, -9)	(0, -6)

To see the design, you will need **1 color**.

Color the **squares** with the following coordinates:

1. (-6, -6)   (-6, -3)   (-3, -3)   (-3, -6)
2. (-6, 3)   (-6, 6)   (-3, 6)   (-3, 3)
3. (3, 3)   (3, 6)   (6, 6)   (6, 3)
4. (3, -3)   (3, -6)   (6, -6)   (6, -3)

Color the **triangles** with the following coordinates:

1. (-3, 6)   (-3, 9)   (0, 6)
2. (0, 6)   (3, 6)   (3, 9)
3. (3, 6)   (6, 6)   (6, 9)
4. (6, 3)   (6, 6)   (9, 6)
5. (6, 3)   (6, 0)   (9, 3)
6. (6, 0)   (6, -3)   (9, -3)
7. (6, -3)   (6, -6)   (9, -6)
8. (3, -6)   (6, -6)   (6, -9)
9. (0, -6)   (3, -6)   (3, -9)
10. (0, -6)   (-3, -9)   (-3, -6)
11. (-3, -6)   (-6, -9)   (-6, -6)
12. (-6, -3)   (-6, -6)   (-9, -6)
13. (-6, -3)   (-9, -3)   (-6, 0)
14. (-6, 0)   (-9, 3)   (-6, 3)
15. (-6, 3)   (-6, 6)   (-9, 6)
16. (-6, 6)   (-6, 9)   (-3, 6)
17. (-3, 6)   (3, 6)   (0, 3)
18. (6, 3)   (3, 0)   (6, -3)
19. (-3, -6)   (0, -3)   (3, -6)
20. (-6, 3)   (-3, 0)   (-6, -3)

The finished design is a traditional quilt block called **Memory**.

Pieced Box

Directions: Find the coordinates indicated below. Work in order, from A to T, connecting each set of points with a straight edge as you go. DO NOT skip around. Use a pencil.

	Connect (X, Y)	To (X, Y)
A	(-10, 10)	(10, 10)
B	(-10, -10)	(10, -10)
C	(-10, -10)	(-10, 10)
D	(10, -10)	(10, 10)
E	(-10, 0)	(0, 10)
F	(0, 10)	(10, 0)
G	(10, 0)	(0, -10)
H	(0, -10)	(-10, 0)
I	(0, 5)	(-5, 0)
J	(0, 5)	(5, 0)

	Connect (X, Y)	To (X, Y)
K	(-5, 0)	(0, -5)
L	(5, 0)	(0, -5)
M	(5, -5)	(10, -10)
N	(-10, -10)	(-5, -5)
O	(5, 5)	(5, -5)
P	(-10, 10)	(-5, 5)
Q	(-5, 5)	(-5, -5)
R	(-5, -5)	(5, -5)
S	(-5, 5)	(5, 5)
T	(10, 10)	(5, 5)

To see the design, you will need **2 colors**.

Use **color #1** to color the **triangles** with the following coordinates:

1. (-5, 5)   (-10, 0)   (-10, 10)
2. (-5, 5)   (0, 10)   (0, 5)
3. (0, 10)   (5, 5)   (10, 10)
4. (5, 0)   (5, 5)   (10, 0)
5. (5, -5)   (10, 0)   (10, -10)
6. (0, -5)   (5, -5)   (0, -10)
7. (-5, -5)   (0, -10)   (-10, -10)
8. (-5, 0)   (-5, -5)   (-10, 0)
9. (-5, 0)   (0, 5)   (5, 0)
10. (-5, 0)   (0, -5)   (5, 0)

Use **color #2** to color the **triangles** with the following coordinates:

1. (-5, 0)   (-5, -5)   (0, -5)
2. (0, -10)   (-5, -5)   (0, -5)
3. (0, -10)   (10, -10)   (5, -5)
4. (5, 5)   (5, 0)   (0, 5)
5. (0, 10)   (0, 5)   (5, 5)
6. (-10, 10)   (0, 10)   (-5, 5)

The finished design is a traditional quilt block called **Pieced Box**.

Pinwheel

Directions: Find the points indicated below. Work in order, from A to N, connecting each set of points with a straight edge as you go. DO NOT skip around. Use a pencil.

	Connect (X, Y)	To (X, Y)
A	(-10, 10)	(10, 10)
B	(-10, -10)	(10, -10)
C	(-10, 10)	(-10, -10)
D	(10, -10)	(10, 10)
E	(-7, 7)	(7, -7)
F	(-7, -7)	(7, 7)
G	(0, 7)	(7, 7)
H	(5, 5)	(10, 0)
I	(7, 0)	(7, -7)
J	(5, -5)	(0, -10)
K	(-7, -7)	(0, -7)
L	(-5, -5)	(-10, 0)
M	(-7, 0)	(-7, 7)
N	(-5, 5)	(0, 10)

To see the design, you will need **2 colors**.

Use **color #1** to color the **triangles** with the following coordinates:

1. (0, 0)   (0, 7)   (7, 7)
2. (0, 0)   (7, 0)   (7, -7)
3. (0, 0)   (0, -7)   (-7, -7)
4. (0, 0)   (-7, 0)   (-7, 7)

Use **color #2** to color the **triangles** with the following coordinates:

1. (0, 0)   (5, 5)   (10, 0)
2. (0, 0)   (5, -5)   (0, -10)
3. (0, 0)   (-5, -5)   (-10, 0)
4. (0, 0)   (-5, 5)   (0, 10)

The finished design is a traditional quilt block called **Pinwheel**.

Sawtooth Square

Directions: Find the coordinates indicated below. Work in order, from A to M, connecting each set of points with a straight edge as you go. DO NOT skip around. Use a pencil.

	Connect (X, Y)	To (X, Y)
A	(-9, -9)	(-9, 9)
B	(-9, 9)	(9, 9)
C	(9, 9)	(9, -9)
D	(9, -9)	(-9, -9)
E	(-3, 9)	(-3, -9)
F	(3, 9)	(3, -9)
G	(-9, 3)	(9, 3)

	Connect (X, Y)	To (X, Y)
H	(-9, -3)	(9, -3)
I	(-3, -9)	(9, 3)
J	(-9, -3)	(-3, -9)
K	(-9, 3)	(-3, -3)
L	(-3, 9)	(3, 3)
M	(3, 9)	(9, 3)

To see the design, you will need **2 colors**.

Use **color #1** to color the **triangles** with the following coordinates:

1. (-9, -9)   (-9, -3)   (-3, -9)
2. (-9, -3)   (-9, 3)   (-3, -3)
3. (-3, 9)   (3, 9)   (3, 3)
4. (3, 9)   (9, 9)   (9, 3)
5. (-3, -9)   (-3, 3)   (9, 3)

Use **color #1** to color the **square** with the following coordinates:

1. (-9, 3)   (-9, 9)   (-3, 9)   (-3, 3)

Use **color #2** to color the **square** with the following coordinates:

1. (3, -9)   (3, -3)   (9, -3)   (9, -9)

Use **color #2** to color the **triangles** with the following coordinates:

1. (-3, -9)   (3, -3)   (3, -9)
2. (-9, -3)   (-3, -3)   (-3, -9)
3. (-9, 3)   (-3, 3)   (-3, -3)
4. (3, -3)   (9, 3)   (9, -3)
5. (-3, 3)   (-3, 9)   (3, 3)
6. (3, 3)   (3, 9)   (9, 3)

The finished design is a traditional quilt block called **Sawtooth Square**.

Solomon's Star

Directions: Find the coordinates indicated below. Work in order, from A to N, connecting each set of points with a straight edge as you go. DO NOT skip around. Use a pencil.

	Connect (X, Y)	To (X, Y)
A	(-8, 8)	(-8, -8)
B	(-8, -8)	(8, -8)
C	(8, -8)	(8, 8)
D	(-8, 8)	(8, 8)
E	(-4, 8)	(-4, -8)
F	(4, 8)	(4, -8)
G	(-8, 4)	(8, 4)

	Connect (X, Y)	To (X, Y)
H	(-8, -4)	(8, -4)
I	(-4, 8)	(8, -4)
J	(-8, 4)	(4, -8)
K	(-8, -4)	(4, 8)
L	(-4, -8)	(8, 4)
M	(-2, 2)	(2, -2)
N	(2, 2)	(-2, -2)

To see the design, you will need **2 colors**.

Use **color #1** to color the **triangles** with the following coordinates:

1. (-4, 8)   (-4, 4)   (0, 4)
2. (4, 4)   (4, 8)   (0, 4)
3. (-8, 4)   (-4, 4)   (-4, 0)
4. (4, 0)   (4, 4)   (8, 4)
5. (-4, 0)   (-4, -4)   (-8, -4)
6. (4, 0)   (4, -4)   (8, -4)
7. (-4, -4)   (-4, -8)   (0, -4)
8. (0, -4)   (4, -4)   (4, -8)
9. (0, 0)   (0, 4)   (-2, 2)
10. (0, 0)   (2, 2)   (4, 0)
11. (-4, 0)   (0, 0)   (-2, -2)
12. (0, 0)   (2, -2)   (0, -4)

Use **color #2** to color the **triangles** with the following coordinates:

1. (-4, 0)   (-4, 4)   (0, 4)
2. (0, 4)   (4, 4)   (4, 0)
3. (-4, 0)   (-4, -4)   (0, -4)
4. (0, -4)   (4, -4)   (4, 0)

The finished design is a traditional quilt block called **Solomon's Star**.

Southern Belle

Directions: Find the coordinates indicated below. Work in order, from A to L, connecting each set of points with a straight edge as you go. DO NOT skip around. Use a pencil.

	Connect (X, Y)	To (X, Y)
A	(-8, 8)	(-8, -8)
B	(-8, -8)	(8, -8)
C	(8, -8)	(8, 8)
D	(-8, 8)	(8, 8)
E	(-8, 0)	(0, 8)
F	(0, 8)	(8, 0)
G	(8, 0)	(0, -8)
H	(0, -8)	(-8, 0)
I	(-8, 8)	(-4, 4)
J	(8, 8)	(4, 4)
K	(8, -8)	(4, -4)
L	(-8, -8)	(-4, -4)

To see the design, you will need **3 colors**.

Use **color #1** to color the **triangles** with the following coordinates:

1. (-8, -8)   (-4, -4)   (0, -8)
2. (-8, 0)   (0, 0)   (0, -8)
3. (0, 0)   (8, 0)   (0, 8)
4. (4, 4)   (0, 8)   (8, 8)

Use **color #2** to color the **triangles** with the following coordinates:

1. (0, -8)   (4, -4)   (8, -8)
2. (-8, 8)   (-4, 4)   (0, 8)

Use **color #3** to color the **triangles** with the following coordinates:

1. (-8, 0)   (-4, -4)   (-8, -8)
2. (4, 4)   (8, 8)   (0, 8)

The finished design is a traditional quilt block called **Southern Belle**.

Starflower

Directions: Find the coordinates indicated below. Work in order, from A to R, connecting each set of points with a straight edge as you go. DO NOT skip around. Use a pencil.

	Connect (X, Y)	To (X, Y)
A	(-8, -8)	(-8, 8)
B	(-8, 8)	(8, 8)
C	(8, 8)	(8, -8)
D	(8, -8)	(-8, -8)
E	(-4, 8)	(-4, -8)
F	(4, 8)	(4, -8)

	Connect (X, Y)	To (X, Y)
G	(-8, 4)	(8, 4)
H	(-8, -4)	(8, -4)
I	(-4, 4)	(4, -4)
J	(-4, -4)	(4, 4)
K	(-4, 8)	(0, 4)
L	(0, 4)	(4, 8)

	Connect (X, Y)	To (X, Y)
M	(8, 4)	(4, 0)
N	(4, 0)	(8, -4)
O	(-4, -8)	(0, -4)
P	(0, -4)	(4, -8)
Q	(-8, -4)	(-4, 0)
R	(-4, 0)	(-8, 4)

To see the design, you will need **2 colors**.

Use **color #1** to color the **triangles** with the following coordinates:

1. (-4, 8)   (0, 4)   (-4, 4)
2. (-4, 4)   (0, 0)   (0, 4)
3. (0, 0)   (4, 0)   (4, 4)
4. (4, 4)   (8, 4)   (4, 0)
5. (0, 0)   (0, -4)   (4, -4)
6. (0, -4)   (4, -4)   (4, -8)
7. (-4, 0)   (-4, -4)   (-8, -4)
8. (-4, 0)   (0, 0)   (-4, -4)

Use **color #2** to color the **triangles** with the following coordinates:

1. (-8, 4)   (-4, 4)   (-4, 0)
2. (-4, 0)   (-4, 4)   (0, 0)
3. (0, 0)   (0, 4)   (4, 4)
4. (0, 4)   (4, 8)   (4, 4)
5. (0, 0)   (-4, -4)   (0, -4)
6. (-4, -4)   (-4, -8)   (0, -4)
7. (0, 0)   (4, 0)   (4, -4)
8. (4, 0)   (4, -4)   (8, -4)

The finished design is a traditional quilt block called **Starflower**.

Streak of Lightning

Directions: Find the coordinates indicated below. Work in order, from A to L, connecting each set of points with a straight edge as you go. DO NOT skip around. Use a pencil.

	Connect (X, Y)	To (X, Y)
A	(-9, 9)	(-9, -9)
B	(-9, -9)	(9, -9)
C	(9, -9)	(9, 9)
D	(-9, 9)	(9, 9)
E	(-6, 9)	(-6, -9)
F	(-3, 9)	(-3, -9)
G	(3, 9)	(3, -9)
H	(6, 9)	(6, -9)
I	(-9, 6)	(9, 6)
J	(-9, 3)	(9, 3)
K	(-9, -3)	(9, -3)
L	(-9, -6)	(9, -6)

To see the design, you will need **1 color**.

Color the **squares** with the following coordinates:

1. (-9, 0)   (-9, 3)   (-6, 0)   (-6, 3)
2. (6, 9)   (9, 9)   (9, 6)   (6, 6)
3. (3, -6)   (6, -6)   (6, -9)   (3, -9)

Color the **rectangles** with the following coordinates:

1. (-9, 3)   (-9, 6)   (-3, 6)   (-3, 3)
2. (-6, 6)   (-6, 9)   (0, 9)   (0, 6)
3. (6, -3)   (6, -9)   (9, -9)   (9, -3)
4. (-9, -6)   (-9, -9)   (-3, -9)   (-3, -6)
5. (-6, -3)   (-6, -6)   (0, -6)   (0, -3)
6. (-3, 0)   (-3, -3)   (3, -3)   (3, 0)
7. (0, 0)   (0, 3)   (6, 3)   (6, 0)
8. (3, 3)   (3, 6)   (9, 6)   (9, 3)

The finished design is a traditional quilt block called **Streak of Lightning**.

Tam's Patch

Directions: Find the coordinates indicated below. Work in order, from A to H, connecting each set of points with a straight edge as you go. DO NOT skip around. Use a pencil.

	Connect (X, Y)	To (X, Y)
A	(-8, -8)	(-8, 8)
B	(-8, 8)	(8, 8)
C	(8, 8)	(8, -8)
D	(8, -8)	(-8, -8)
E	(-8, 4)	(0, 4)
F	(0, -4)	(8, -4)
G	(-4, 4)	(-4, 0)
H	(4, 0)	(4, -4)

To see the design, you will need **3 colors**.

Use **color #1** to color the **squares** with the following coordinates:

1. (-8, -8)   (-8, 0)   (0, 0)   (0, -8)
2. (0, 0)   (0, 8)   (8, 8)   (8, 0)

Use **color #2** to color the **squares** with the following coordinates:

1. (-4, 0)   (-4, 4)   (0, 4)   (0, 0)
2. (0, 0)   (4, 0)   (4, -4)   (0, -4)

Use **color #3** to color the **squares** with the following coordinates:

1. (-8, 0)   (-8, 4)   (-4, 4)   (-4, 0)
2. (4, -4)   (4, 0)   (8, 0)   (8, -4)

Use **color #3** to color the **rectangles** with the following coordinates:

1. (-8, 4)   (-8, 8)   (0, 8)   (0, 4)
2. (0, -4)   (8, -4)   (8, -8)   (0, -8)

The finished design is a traditional quilt block called **Tam's Patch**.

The Wishing Ring

Directions: Find the coordinates indicated below. Work in order, from A to T, connecting each set of points with a straight edge as you go. DO NOT skip around. Use a pencil.

	Connect (X, Y)	To (X, Y)
A	(-10, 10)	(10, 10)
B	(-10, 10)	(-10, -10)
C	(-10, -10)	(10, -10)
D	(10, 10)	(10, -10)
E	(-6, 10)	(-6, -10)
F	(-2, 10)	(-2, -10)
G	(2, 10)	(2, -10)

	Connect (X, Y)	To (X, Y)
H	(6, 10)	(6, -10)
I	(-10, 6)	(10, 6)
J	(-10, 2)	(10, 2)
K	(-10, -2)	(10, -2)
L	(-10, -6)	(10, -6)
M	(-10, 6)	(-6, 10)
N	(6, 10)	(10, 6)

	Connect (X, Y)	To (X, Y)
O	(10, -6)	(6, -10)
P	(-10, -6)	(-6, -10)
Q	(-6, 2)	(-2, 6)
R	(2, 6)	(6, 2)
S	(6, -2)	(2, -6)
T	(-6, -2)	(-2, -6)

To see the design, you will need **1 color**.

Color the **squares** with the following coordinates:

1. (-6, 10)   (-2, 10)   (-2, 6)   (-6, 6)
2. (2, 10)   (6, 10)   (6, 6)   (2, 6)
3. (-10, 6)   (-6, 6)   (-6, 2)   (-10, 2)
4. (6, 6)   (10, 6)   (10, 2)   (6, 2)
5. (-6, 2)   (-2, 2)   (-2, -2)   (-6, -2)

6. (2, 2)   (6, 2)   (6, -2)   (2, -2)
7. (-10, -2)   (-6, -2)   (-6, -6)   (-10, -6)
8. (6, -2)   (10, -2)   (10, -6)   (6, -6)
9. (-6, -6)   (-2, -6)   (-2, -10) (-6, -10)
10. (2, -6)   (6, -6)   (6, -10)   (2, -10)

Color the **triangles** with the following coordinates:

1. (-10, 6)   (-10, 10)   (-6, 10)
2. (6, 10)   (10, 10)   (10, 6)
3. (-10, -6)   (-10, -10)   (-6, -10)
4. (6, -10)   (10, -10)   (10, -6)

Color the **trapezoids** with the following coordinates:

1. (-6, 2)   (-2, 6)   (2, 6)   (6, 2)
2. (-6, -2)   (6, -2)   (2, -6)   (-2, -6)

The finished design is a traditional quilt block called **The Wishing Ring**.

Tudor Rose

Directions: Find the coordinates indicated below. Work in order, from A to BB, connecting each set of points with a straight edge as you go. DO NOT skip around. Use a pencil.

	Connect (X, Y)	To (X, Y)
A	(-10, 10)	(10, 10)
B	(-10, 10)	(-10, -10)
C	(-10, -10)	(10, -10)
D	(10, 10)	(10, -10)
E	(0, 10)	(-10, 0)
F	(-10, 0)	(0, -10)
G	(0, -10)	(10, 0)
H	(10, 0)	(0, 10)
I	(-6, 4)	(4, -6)
J	(-4, 6)	(6, -4)

	Connect (X, Y)	To (X, Y)
K	(4, 6)	(-6, -4)
L	(6, 4)	(-4, -6)
M	(-6, 1)	(-7, 0)
N	(-7, 0)	(-6, -1)
O	(-6, -1)	(-5, 0)
P	(-5, 0)	(-6, 1)
Q	(0, 7)	(-1, 6)
R	(-1, 6)	(0, 5)
S	(0, 5)	(1, 6)

	Connect (X, Y)	To (X, Y)
T	(1, 6)	(0, 7)
U	(6, 1)	(5, 0)
V	(5, 0)	(6, -1)
W	(6, -1)	(7, 0)
X	(7, 0)	(6, 1)
Y	(0, -5)	(-1, -6)
Z	(-1, -6)	(0, -7)
AA	(0, -7)	(1, -6)
BB	(1, -6)	(0, -5)

To see the design, you will need **1 color**.

Color the **triangles** with the following coordinates:

1. (-10, 10)   (-10, 0)   (0, 10)
2. (0, 10)   (10, 10)   (10, 0)
3. (10, 0)   (10, -10)   (0, -10)
4. (-10, 0)   (0, -10)   (-10, -10)

Color the **rectangles** with the following coordinates:

1. (-6, 4)   (-4, 6)   (0, 2)   (-2, 0)
2. (0, 2)   (2, 0)   (6, 4)   (4, 6)
3. (2, 0)   (0, -2)   (4, -6)   (6, -4)
4. (-6, -4)   (-4, -6)   (0, -2)   (-2, 0)

Color the **rhombuses** with the following coordinates:

1. (0, 7)   (1, 6)   (0, 5)   (-1, 6)
2. (-7, 0)   (-6, 1)   (-5, 0)   (-6, -1)
3. (5, 0)   (6, 1)   (7, 0)   (6, -1)
4. (0, -5)   (1, -6)   (0, -7)   (-1, -6)

The finished design is a traditional quilt block called **Tudor Rose**.

Tulip Lady Fingers

Directions: Find the coordinates indicated below. Work in order, from A to X, connecting each set of points with a straight edge as you go. DO NOT skip around. Use a pencil.

	Connect (X, Y)	To (X, Y)
A	(-9, 9)	(-9, -9)
B	(-9, -9)	(9, -9)
C	(9, -9)	(9, 9)
D	(-9, 9)	(9, 9)
E	(-3, 9)	(-3, -9)
F	(3, 9)	(3, -9)
G	(-9, 3)	(9, 3)
H	(-9, -3)	(9, -3)

	Connect (X, Y)	To (X, Y)
I	(-6, 3)	(-6, 9)
J	(-9, 6)	(-3, 6)
K	(6, 3)	(6, 9)
L	(3, 6)	(9, 6)
M	(-6, -3)	(-6, -9)
N	(-9, -6)	(-3, -6)
O	(3, -6)	(9, -6)
P	(6, -3)	(6, -9)

	Connect (X, Y)	To (X, Y)
Q	(-9, 6)	(-6, 3)
R	(6, 3)	(9, 6)
S	(3, -6)	(6, -9)
T	(-6, -9)	(-3, -6)
U	(-6, 9)	(-3, 6)
V	(3, 6)	(6, 9)
W	(6, -3)	(9, -6)
X	(-9, -6)	(-6, -3)

To see the design, you will need **2 colors**.

Use **color #1** to color the **triangles** with the following coordinates:

1. (-9, 6)   (-6, 6)   (-6, 3)
2. (6, 3)   (6, 6)   (9, 6)
3. (-6, -6)   (-3, -6)   (-6, -9)
4. (3, -6)   (6, -6)   (6, -9)
5. (-6, 9)   (-6, 6)   (-3, 6)
6. (3, 6)   (6, 6)   (6, 9)
7. (-6, -6)   (-6, -3)   (-9, -6)
8. (6, -3)   (6, -6)   (9, -6)

Use **color #2** to color the **squares** with the following coordinates:

1. (-3, 3)   (3, 3)   (3, -3)   (-3, -3)
2. (-6, 6)   (-6, 3)   (-3, 6)   (-3, 3)
3. (3, 3)   (3, 6)   (6, 6)   (6, 3)
4. (-6, -3)   (-3, -3)   (-3, -6)   (-6, -6)
5. (3, -3)   (3, -6)   (6, -3)   (6, -6)

The finished design is a traditional quilt block called **Tulip Lady Fingers**.

Wandering Star

Directions: Find the coordinates indicated below. Work in order, from A to R, connecting each set of points with a straight edge as you go. DO NOT skip around. Use a pencil.

	Connect (X, Y)	To (X, Y)
A	(-9, 9)	(-9, -9)
B	(-9, -9)	(9, -9)
C	(9, -9)	(9, 9)
D	(-9, 9)	(9, 9)
E	(-3, 9)	(-3, -9)
F	(3, 9)	(3, -9)
G	(-9, 3)	(9, 3)
H	(-9, 3)	(-3, -3)
I	(-9, -3)	(9, -3)

	Connect (X, Y)	To (X, Y)
J	(-3, 3)	(3, -3)
K	(-3, -3)	(3, 3)
L	(-3, 3)	(3, 9)
M	(-9, 3)	(-3, 9)
N	(3, 9)	(9, 3)
O	(3, 3)	(9, -3)
P	(9, -3)	(3, -9)
Q	(3, -3)	(-3, -9)
R	(-3, -9)	(-9, -3)

To see the design, you will need **2 colors**.

Use **color #1** to color the **triangles** with the following coordinates:

1. (-9, 3)   (-9, 9)   (-3, 9)
2. (-3, 3)   (3, 9)   (3, 3)
3. (-3, 3)   (3, 3)   (0, 0)
4. (3, -9)   (9, -9)   (9, -3)
5. (0, 0)   (3, -3)   (-3, -3)
6. (-3, -3)   (-3, -9)   (3, -3)

Use **color #2** to color the **triangles** with the following coordinates:

1. (0, 0)   (-3, 3)   (-3, -3)
2. (0, 0)   (3, 3)   (3, -3)
3. (3, 3)   (9, -3)   (3, -3)
4. (-9, -3)   (-9, -9)   (-3, -9)
5. (-3, -3)   (-9, 3)   (-3, 3)
6. (3, 9)   (9, 3)   (9, 9)

The finished design is a traditional quilt block called **Wandering Star**.

Solutions

Alaska Homestead, page 7

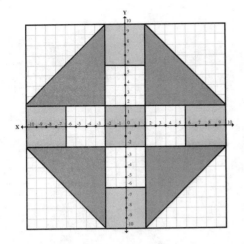

Blazing Arrows, page 10

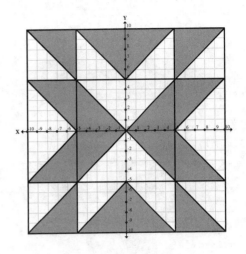

Anvil, page 8

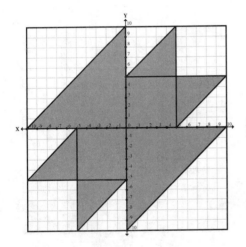

Broken Arrows, page 11

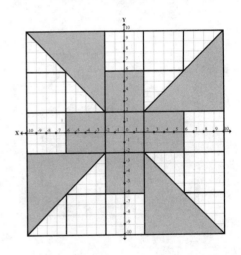

At the Square, page 9

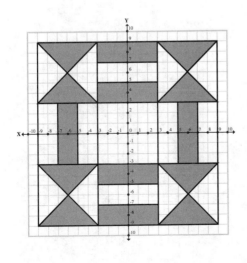

Chevron, page 12

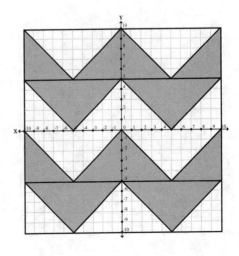

Solutions

Churn Dash, page 13

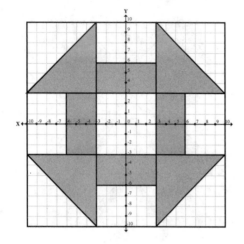

Crazy Anne, page 16

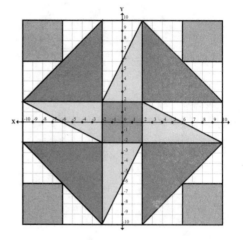

Colonial Pavement, page 14

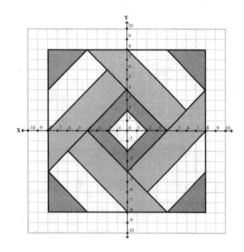

Crossed Roads, page 17

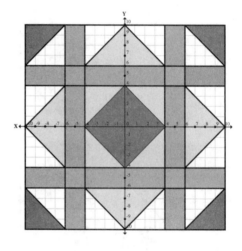

Country Checkers, page 15

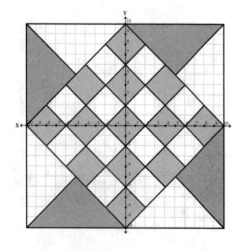

Double Quartet, page 18

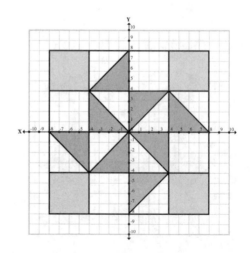

Solutions

Dove in a Window, page 19

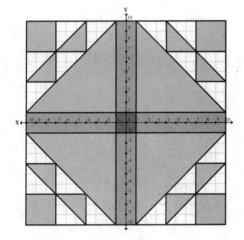

Fool's Square, page 22

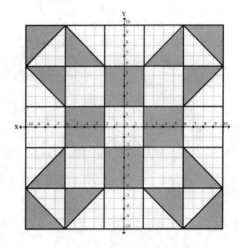

Dutch Nine Patch, page 20

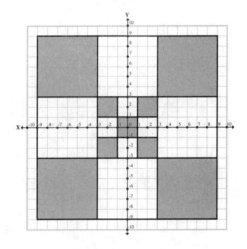

Four Goblets, page 23

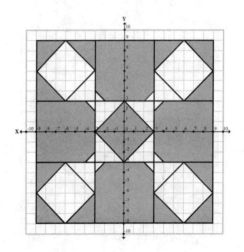

Dutchman's Puzzle, page 21

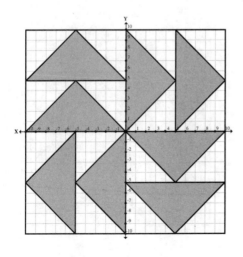

Framed Four Patch, page 24

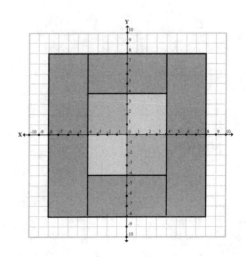

Solutions

Fruit Basket, page 25

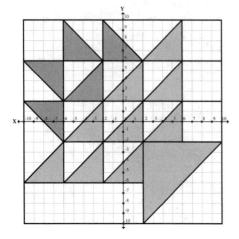

Hill and Valley, page 28

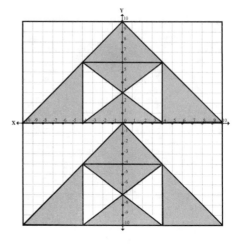

Grandmother's Puzzle, page 26

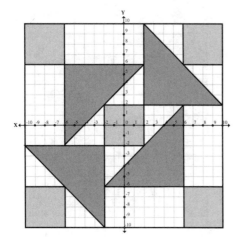

Interlocked Squares, page 29

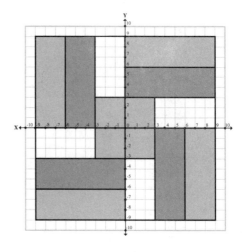

Hearth and Home, page 27

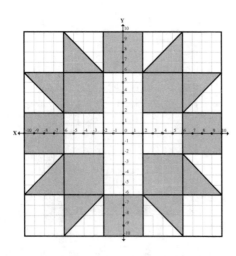

Memory, page 30

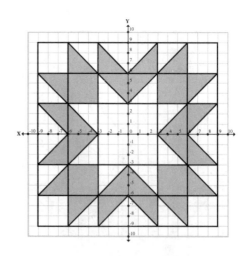

Solutions

Pieced Box, page 31

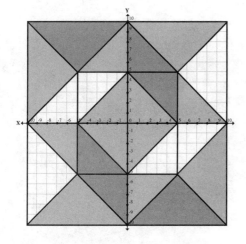

Solomon's Star, page 34

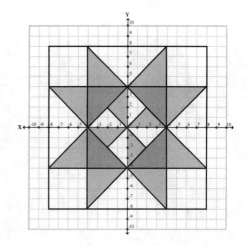

Pinwheel, page 32

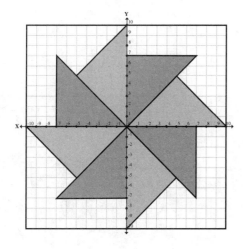

Southern Belle, page 35

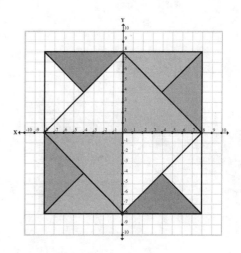

Sawtooth Square, page 33

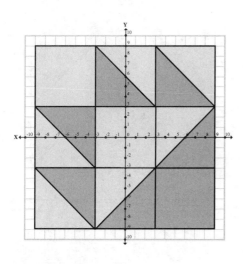

Starflower, page 36

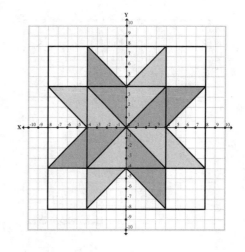

Solutions

Streak of Lightning, page 37

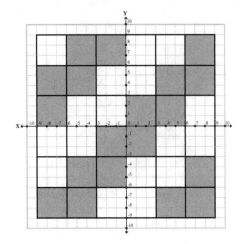

Tudor Rose, page 40

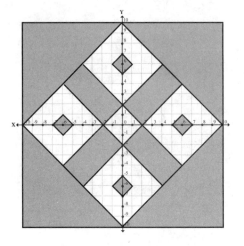

Tam's Patch, page 38

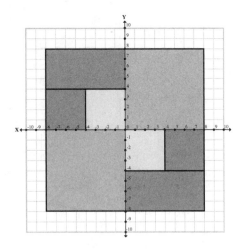

Tulip Lady Fingers, page 41

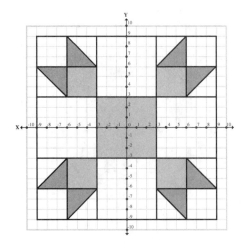

The Wishing Ring, page 39

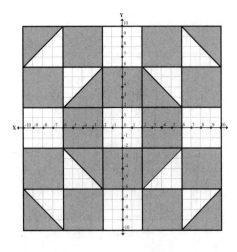

Wandering Star, page 42

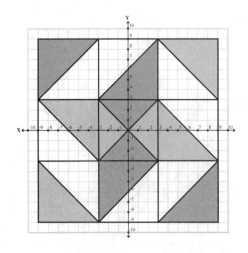